Putting the Record Straight

WHAT COMES TO MIND when you hear someone talking about Christianity? Perhaps you think of people who go around bashing other people with their Bible! Perhaps you have a vague recollection of a man called Jesus Christ who lived in Palestine thousands of years ago? Or maybe Christianity makes you think of endless church services with long sermons?

Well, here's news for you. Being a Christian is none of these things. Being a Christian is about having an active, personal relationship with the Almighty, living God.

Back to the beginning

You don't have to look far to realise that today's world is full of problems: greed, selfishness, hunger, war, terrorism, hate, broken relationships and more. Throughout the world, there are people doing their best to improve the situation but their efforts only seem to scratch the surface. Have things always been this bad? What is the root cause of these problems?

Here's the bad news. We're the problem. When God created the world, He created a perfect place. He created men and women to live in the world under His authority and enjoy a fulfilled personal relationship with Him.

Know that the Lord is God.
It is He who made us, and we are his;
we are his people, the sheep of his pasture.

(Psalm 100:3)

But God doesn't force us into this relationship. He lets us choose. He gives us the free will to choose whether to accept or reject Him, to choose whether to accept or reject His commandments.

Maybe you have never consciously accepted or rejected God. Maybe you have.

Life on the Big Screen

Imagine the whole of your life projected on to a massive screen in front of you. The film shows every single aspect of your life – everything you have ever done, said or even thought. Nothing is omitted. I wonder how you would feel about watching that film – especially in the presence of everybody else involved!

You might feel like the man in court who, pleading innocence, listens for several hours to the court proceedings and then shouts, "I'm guilty!" The judge turns to him and says, "Why didn't you say that several hours ago?" "Well," replies the man, "I didn't realise I was guilty until I heard all the evidence!" Often we go through life thinking we haven't done anything wrong – until we stop to examine the evidence.

God's Commandments

How do you view God's commandments? As out-of-date,

irrelevant rules and restrictions that stop us having fun – or as wise instructions on how to live in harmony with God and with each other?

Here are God's Ten Commandments in modern English. Have you ever taken them seriously?

1. Have you always put God at the centre of your life, where He ought to be?

2. Have you ever put anything or anyone else in the place of God in your life?

3. Have you ever used the Name of God carelessly or insincerely?

4. Have you always kept one day each week for worshipping God and for rest?

5. Have you always respected and honoured your parents?

6. Have you ever murdered anyone – or even hated anyone?

7. Have you ever committed adultery? Have you ever had impure or lustful thoughts about another person?

8. Have you ever stolen anything? What about another person's reputation?

9. Have you ever told a lie or half-truth to another person or about another person?

10. Have you ever been jealous of what is not yours?

(Exodus 20 and Matthew 5)

Failure to keep these instructions that God has given us is called sin and it affects everybody.

Anyone, then, who knows the good
he ought to do and doesn't do it, sins.

(James 4:17)

"Sin" is a word that has lost its true meaning. Because we use the word "sin" lightly, we don't take its reality seriously. Most people think sin doesn't matter, or that it is quite fun.

Breakdown in Communication

God, however, does take sin seriously. When we ignore God's instructions, we are ignoring Him. We are turning our backs on Him and rejecting Him.

Because God is perfect, He can't tolerate our sin and so it creates a barrier between us and Him. It prevents us from having the loving, personal relationship He wants us to have with Him.

The Lord saw how great man's wickedness on the
earth had become, and that every inclination of the
thoughts of his heart was only evil all the time. The
Lord was grieved that he had made man on the
earth, and his heart was filled with pain.

(Genesis 6:5-6)

When there is a breakdown between two parties, a mediator is often brought in to represent the two sides and bring them back together. We have a breakdown between us and God, but who is qualified to represent both God and mankind? Only someone who is both God *and* human.

Jesus Christ, the Son of God, came into the world as a human to restore communication between us and God and to give us a new relationship with Him.

For Christ died for sins once for all, the righteous for the unrighteous, to bring you to God.

(1 Peter 3:18)

Facing Punishment

God is life and light.
Remove life and death results.
Remove light and darkness is left.

Think back to that man in the courtroom. Having heard all the evidence, the judge pronounces his judgment: "Guilty". And the punishment – the maximum fine. The man just stands there in the dock, shocked at the severity of the sentence. Then suddenly, the judge comes down from his seat, walks over to the man and hands him a cheque for the full amount of the fine.

In the same way, God judges our lives. He looks at all our thoughts, words and actions. He weighs up the evidence and pronounces His judgment: "Guilty". Guilty of turning our back on God, and failing to live by His instructions. And the punishment – separation from Him, not only now but for eternity.

He will punish those who do not know God and do not obey the gospel of our Lord Jesus. They will be punished with everlasting destruction and shut out from the presence of the Lord and from the majesty of his power.
(2 Thessalonians 1:8-9)

But, having judged us, God then acts to save us from serving that eternal sentence by sending His only Son, Jesus Christ, to take the punishment we deserve. Jesus died on a cross and, because He died, we don't have to face the punishment for our sin. He took our place.

As well as showing us how much God hates sin, this also shows us how much He loves us. God sent His *only* Son. He was the "cheque", signed with His own blood, that puts us right with God.

> *For God so loved the world that he gave his one and only Son, that whoever believes in him shall not perish but have eternal life.*   (John 3:16)

It doesn't end there...

But Christianity does not end with Jesus' funeral.

Imagine you are walking down the street. You reach a point where the road branches into two and you don't know which way to go. Two men are lying there – one is dead and one is alive. Which one would you ask for directions?

Three days after Jesus died on the cross He came back to life again. He is alive today, which means that we can communicate with Him and find direction in our lives.

> *But God raised him from the dead, freeing him from the agony of death, because it was impossible for death to keep its hold on him.*   (Acts 2:24)

Jesus is not physically on earth today but His living Holy Spirit is within every person who has become a Christian. The Holy Spirit guides us and strengthens us and helps us in our relationship with God and with other people.

*When he, the Spirit of truth, comes, he will guide
you into all truth.* (John 16:13)

Becoming a Christian

If you're wondering how your relationship with
God can be restored, then look to Jesus. He is the
only way to God. Jesus said these words:

*I am the way and the truth and
the life. No-one comes to the
Father except through me.*

(John 14:6)

Admit

The first thing to do is
to admit that we are
separated from God
because we have
ignored Him. We need
a mediator who will
step in and mend the
broken relationship between us and
God. We must admit that we deserve
punishment because of our sin.

Commit

As we look at what Jesus did on the cross for
us, we realise that He has taken the punishment we
deserve and has therefore dealt with our sin.

Committing our lives to Jesus Christ brings God's
forgiveness and new life. In the physical world, a new life
is created as soon as conception takes place. In the
spiritual world, new life begins when someone commits
his or her life to Jesus Christ and so receives the Holy
Spirit and the new life Jesus offers. That person is "born
again".

Submit

It is one thing to admit that we have sinned and to begin a new relationship with God by committing our lives to Him. It is quite another thing to continue that relationship and live it out, day by day. Submitting to God involves living as God wants us to live. We must allow God to work in our lives and gradually change us into the kind of person He wants us to be.

God does not leave us to handle this alone. It is not like turning over a new leaf or having a moral clean-up. His Holy Spirit comes into our lives to help us become more like Jesus. Every day, He guides and strengthens us and helps us to serve God.

If you want to begin a new relationship with God, then say these words as a prayer to Jesus, who is the way to God:

Thank you, Jesus, for dying on the cross.

Thank you, Jesus, that I can come to You now because You are alive.

I admit that I have lived my life without You and that I have broken Your laws.

I commit myself to You and I ask for Your forgiveness.

I receive You into my life by Your Holy Spirit.

Help me to submit my life to Your teaching and to your direction from this moment on.

Amen.

The First Step

Asking Jesus into your life is just the first step – like shaking hands with someone you've just met. But getting to know someone well takes time and effort. It is the same with Jesus.

We can get to know Jesus better through the Bible, through prayer and through the local church.

The Bible

The Bible is a library of sixty-six books, in two parts –
the Old Testament and the New Testament. Don't
be tempted to think that only some of the Bible is
relevant. It is God's Word and full of sound and vital
advice!

> *All Scripture is God-breathed and is useful for*
> *teaching, rebuking, correcting and training in*
> *righteousness, so that the man of God may be*
> *thoroughly equipped for every good work.*
>
> (2 Timothy 3:16-17)

The Old Testament teaches us that there is one true God.
It tells us about many different aspects of His character
and shows us how to live in a way that is pleasing to Him.

The New Testament starts with the Gospels.
What Jesus said and did as presented
from different perspectives by four
of his disciples: Matthew, Mark,
Luke and John. Next is the Book
of Acts, which explains how
the Christian Church started
to grow. Then come twenty-one
letters written to churches and
individuals to guide them over
difficulties and misunderstandings.
The last book, Revelation, is an
encouragement to look
beyond the present to
what God has in store
for his people.

Reading and
studying the

Bible, in a modern translation such as the New International Version, will increase your understanding of God. It will help to develop and strengthen your character, and show you the person God wants you to be in today's world.

If you are not very familiar with the Bible, the Gospel of John may be a good place to start. It describes the life of Jesus and some of the amazing things He did. It tells of His death on the cross and how He rose from the dead.

Prayer

Jesus longs for us to have a deep friendship with Him. The key to any friendship is communication and the way that we communicate with Jesus is through prayer. Just as the Bible is God's way of speaking to us, prayer is the way we speak to God. Jesus' twelve disciples asked Him how to pray and He said:

> *This is how you should pray:*
> *'Our Father in heaven,*
> *hallowed be your name,*
> *your kingdom come,*
> *your will be done,*
> *on earth as it is in heaven.*
> *Give us today our daily bread.*
> *Forgive us our debts,*
> *as we also have forgiven our debtors.*
> *And lead us not into temptation,*
> *but deliver us from the evil one.'* (Matthew 6:9-13)

The first three statements of this prayer are all concerned with God and how great He is. It is always good to start our prayers by remembering how great God is and praying that what He wants will be done.

As you do this, you may become conscious of things you have done wrong since you last spoke to Him.

Acknowledge that you may have hurt Him, someone else or even yourself. Say sorry to God and you will receive His forgiveness.

> *If we confess our sins, he (God) is faithful and just and will forgive us our sins and purify us from all unrighteousness.* (1 John 1:9)

Jesus then said, "Give us today our daily bread." Pray about the day ahead and ask God to provide for your basic needs.

"And lead us not into temptation." Pray for God's strength in the various situations that you will find yourself in. Pray for wisdom and insight. Pray for guidance in knowing how to react in those particular situations.

So, spend some time each day praying to God. You don't have to use long or special words, God will always hear you. However, because He knows what's best for us, He does not always answer our prayers in the way we expect. Sometimes God says "yes", sometimes "no" and sometimes the answer is "wait".

> *Seven days without prayer makes one weak.* Anonymous

Church

If you are a Christian, you are part of the family of God. So don't go it alone. Belonging to a church, particularly a small group within it, will bring you regularly in touch with other people who also know Jesus and are part of the same family. They can encourage you – and you can encourage them.

> *Let us not give up meeting together, as some are in the habit of doing, but let us encourage one another.* (Hebrews 10:25)

In a church, you will be able to worship God – to give expression to the joy and thankfulness that is in your heart. And you will be able to receive teaching to stimulate your mind, to inspire you and to nourish you.

The church is not a cruise liner on which we glide to heaven. It is a battleship that requires all hands on deck as it fights its way through life to a tremendous destination. So get involved! As well as joining some kind of small group, why not try to find some way you can help out – Sunday School, the Youth Group, serving coffee or helping those in need?

No Bed of Roses

You may be experiencing a whole range of feelings – or you may be feeling no different at all. It is important to reflect on the implications of the commitment you have made. At some stage, you will need to explain to your friends what you have done.

It will not be long before you realise that you are in a fight. The Christian life is not a bed of roses. The Devil, who is also called Satan, does all he can to ruin our relationship with God. There will be hard times but those hard times produce character and the goal of eternal life with our Heavenly Father makes it all worth it!

> *We also rejoice in our sufferings, because we know that suffering produces perseverance; perseverance, character; and character, hope. And hope does not disappoint us, because God has poured out his love into our hearts by the Holy Spirit, whom he has given us.* (Romans 5:3-5)

So don't give up on reading the Bible, talking to your Heavenly Father and going to church.

Once we have committed our lives to Jesus, we can have complete assurance that our relationship with God is restored. It doesn't depend on our circumstances or on our feelings. As Christians, we base our assurance on three facts:

The Word of God – the Bible
We can be sure that the Bible is true and that God will keep His promises. He will keep His Word and never let us go.

The Work of Christ
We can be sure that, on the cross, Jesus Christ took the punishment for our sin, dealing with it once and for all. His rising from the dead is proof of this.

The Witness of the Holy Spirit
That the Holy Spirit helps us to pray and to call God "Father" is a witness itself.
We can be sure that He will help and protect us and bring us into God's Kingdom.

Those three facts are rather like the legs of a three-legged stool. When all three legs are there, we are secure.

So when you come up against hard times, persevere. Keep on keeping on.

> *I press on towards the goal to win*
> *the prize for which God has called*
> *me heavenwards in Christ Jesus.*
> (Philippians 3:14)

Discover the Christian faith

Many people have false ideas about Christianity
and J. John has devoted his life to putting the
record straight. In these few pages he explains
how to become a Christian.

*"J. John appeals to everyone.
Instant communication."*
CLIFF RICHARD.

Other books by the author from
Hodder and Stoughton:

Life Means What? - the reality of God

Ten Steps to the Good Life - living Christianity

ISBN 0-340-55229-8

00050

9 780340 552292

Price 50p

Emma Donaldson
Cabin Fever

BLACK LACE